THE FORGOTTEN FOOT

A GUIDE TO DEVELOPING FOOT INDEPENDENCE AND HI-HAT/BASS COORDINATION FOR ALL DRUMMERS

BY KOFI BAKER AND JORDAN HILL

Cover photo by Felice Kinnear

ISBN 978-1-4234-8815-6

HAL•LEONARD®
CORPORATION
7777 W. BLUEMOUND RD. P.O. BOX 13819 MILWAUKEE, WI 53213

In Australia Contact:
Hal Leonard Australia Pty. Ltd.
4 Lentara Court
Cheltenham, Victoria, 3192 Australia
Email: ausadmin@halleonard.com.au

Visit Hal Leonard Online at
www.halleonard.com

TABLE OF CONTENTS

CD TRACK LISTING

CD recorded and mixed by Brett Hansen.

Chapter 4 – **SHUFFLE AND JAZZ**

Chapter 5 – **DOUBLE BASS DRUM**

Chapter 6 – **FOOT PATTERNS**

 **PREFACE**

Over the last fifteen years of teaching and twenty-five years of playing in clubs, I have talked to a lot of drummers. Two of the biggest complaints I hear are, "I always slow down or speed up when I am playing a fill," and "I lose track of beat 1 during a solo." Both of these problems can be traced back to one source: the left foot (or the right foot for you left-handers). The left foot seems to have been forgotten by a lot of drummers. Your left foot's primary use is not double bass, it is timekeeping. I think a lot of drummers have the intention of going back and learning four-way coordination after they learn three-way coordination, but it just never happens. That is why left foot coordination needs to be learned from the very beginning.

By learning to keep the quarter-note pulse going with your left foot, your timing and consistency will be greatly increased and you will know where the quarter-note pulse is. Left foot coordination will improve your double bass playing as well. I like to compare it to learning to drive. If you learn to drive using a car with an automatic transmission, you take for granted that the transmission is shifting when it is supposed to on its own. If you ever needed to drive a stick-shift car, you would need to relearn how to drive. When you learn to drive a stick shift, you are responsible for when and how the transmission is shifted, and the transition to driving an automatic transmission is no problem. In the same way, when you learn to play drumset with only three-way coordination, you are taking for granted where the quarter note is. If you want to add the quarter note with your left foot, you will be unable to, without going back and learning the coordination. If, however, from the very beginning you learn to play four-way coordination, you will be that much farther ahead, and your timekeeping will be vastly improved. Everything else you want to play on the drums will be that much easier to grasp because you have learned how to use your forgotten left foot.

ABOUT THE AUTHORS

Kofi Baker

As the son of Cream's legendary drummer, Ginger Baker, Kofi Baker began playing drums at an early age. He first appeared at age six, with his father on the live UK TV show, *The Old Gray Whistle Test*, and has been performing ever since. The early 1980s found Kofi and his father playing drum duets throughout Europe. He also toured the continent with several British bands. Highlights of the 1990s included a Budapest tour with Jack Bruce, recording several albums, and more drum duets with Ginger. Now living in the Los Angeles area, Kofi is currently playing in OHM, a jazz-fusion outfit with Chris Poland (of Megadeth) on guitar. Kofi's latest project is a Cream and Blind Faith tribute band.

Kofi has been teaching drums for the last fifteen years at The Kofi Baker Drum School, and at various drum clinics around the country.

Kofi plays Ludwig and Page drums, a Ford snare, and Peace hardware. He uses Zildjian cymbals, Vater sticks, Aquarian drumheads, E-Pad practice pads, and Avantone microphones with Pro-Klamps, as well as Revolution percussion accessories. Kofi also endorses Sam Ash music stores.

Contact:
kofibaker@hotmail.com
The Kofi Baker Drum School 714-771-2389
www.kofibaker.com

Jordan Hill

Jordan Hill is an author and educator. He lives in Southern California with his wife, daughter, and son. Jordan performs and records with local solo artists. He also teaches privately. Visit Jordan's blog at www.motorrhythms.blogspot.com.

Contact:
jordan.hill@sbcglobal.net

Jordan would like to dedicate this book to Hudson Robert.

1 FUNDAMENTALS

This chapter provides instruction on how to count and read music, and includes some of the most common elements of drumset notation. The exercises included feature foot patterns and accent exercises. These foot patterns start building hi-hat foot coordination from the very beginning. For the drummer that has been playing for a while and is comfortable with counting and reading, this chapter will serve as a good review of the basics. Use the reading and accent pages to build and strengthen hi-hat foot coordination.

The reading and accent pages in this chapter can be used throughout the entire book. They can be used as melody lines for the rock beat pages as well as ideas for fills. They can also be played overtop the foot patterns in Chapter 6. Once the reading and accent pages can be played comfortably, move on to Chapter 2.

DRUMSET NOTATION

Notation Key

The example below is the notation key for this book which utilizes a five-piece drumset: snare drum, bass drum, and three tom toms. The space above the staff can be played either on the hi-hat cymbals or the ride cymbal.

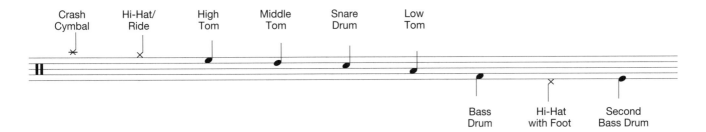

Notation Style

There are multiple methods of writing drumset music. Two of those methods are shown in the following examples. Example A shows the stems of the bass drum and hi-hat (with foot) notes pointing down away from the cymbal and snare notes. Example B shows those same notes pointing up and connecting with the cymbal and snare drum notes. The majority of this book uses the writing style from Example A, where the feet are separated from the hands. There are a few pages in Chapter 3 and Chapter 6 where the feet are connected up to the hands as in Example B.

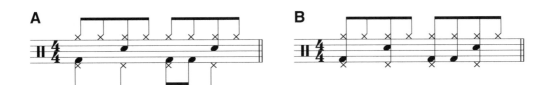

Notes and Rests

Repeat Signs and Symbols

The following example shows an example of *repeat signs*, which indicate to repeat the section of music contained within them. There can be any number of measures between the "start" (right-facing) and "end" (left-facing) repeat signs. (Note: if music repeats back to the beginning, a "start" repeat sign is not necessary.)

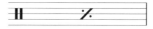

The following is a *measure repeat* symbol, which indicates to repeat the previous measure once. It can also be written across multiple measures. If so, there would be a number above it indicating how many measures to repeat.

Stickings

Throughout the book stickings are used to notate which hand is playing each note. The stickings are written above the staff and directly above the notes they correspond with. This is how the stickings are notated.

R = right hand

L = left hand

Note-Value Tree

The next example shows several different types of note values, and how many of each would fit into one measure of 4/4.

Dotted Notes and Rests

A *dotted* note or rest has a small dot that looks like a period written to the right of it. When a note or rest is dotted, its length is increased by half of its original value. For example, if a half note receives two quarter-note beats, a dotted half note is worth three quarter notes. A dotted quarter note is worth one-and-a-half beats, or three eighth notes, and so on. This is also true of dotted rests. The following example shows several types of dotted notes and their value.

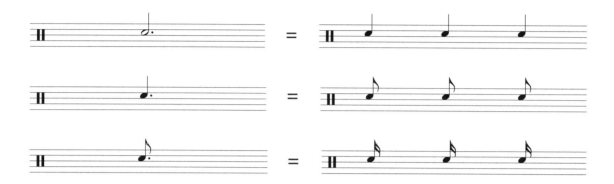

Time Signatures

Time signatures indicate how many beats are in a measure, as well as what kind of note receives a beat. A time signature is like a fraction: the bottom number determines what kind of note gets the beat, and the top number shows how many of those notes are in a measure. The most common time signature is 4/4. The method in which notes are counted differs, based on the time signature. In 4/4, quarter notes are counted "1, 2, 3, 4," but in 6/8, eighth notes may be counted "1, 2, 3, 4, 5, 6."

Keeping this in mind, the following is true:

- A number "2" on the bottom means that the half note gets the beat.
- A number "4" on the bottom means that the quarter note gets the beat.
- A number "8" on the bottom means that the eighth note gets the beat.

TEMPO

Tempo means "speed." It is measured in beats per minute, or "BPM," and indicates the speed of the beat (or pulse) of the music. Metronomes have BPM markings ranging from slow to fast. The tempo "60 BPM" is equal to one beat per second, and thus "120 BPM" is equal to two beats per second. It is important to use a metronome while practicing in order to maintain a consistent tempo. Always learn to play a new exercise at a slower tempo, and gradually speed up the tempo as you become more confident with the exercise. Tempo markings are usually found at the beginning of a piece of music. The example below shows what a tempo marking might look like. A word indicating speed may be followed by a *metronomic marking* indicating the precise speed measured in "beats per minute."

Moderately Fast (♩ = 120)

COUNTING

Counting is the starting point for learning any new rhythm or piece of music. With the ability to count music, even the most difficult rhythms can be learned. Count out loud while playing the following examples. It is also recommended you continue to count out loud when learning any exercise.

The most basic counting involves the quarter-note beat. In a 4/4 measure, quarter notes are counted "one, two, three, four."

The quarter note can be subdivided into eighth notes and sixteenth notes. In this book, *eighth notes* which occur in between the beat are notated with a "+" sign, which stands for "and" (eighth notes on the beat are counted with the beat number). They are counted "one-and, two-and, three-and, four-and" (Example A). *Sixteenth notes* are written with an "e" and an "a," plus the beat number and the "and" halfway between the beat. Sixteenth notes are counted "one-e-and-a, two-e-and-a, three-e-and-a, four-e-and-a" (Example B).

Quarter notes can also be subdivided into eighth-note triplets and sixteenth-note triplets. *Triplets* can be counted several different ways. They may be broken into three syllables: "tri-pl-et, tri-pl-et," or simply counted: "1-2-3, 1-2-3." Sixteenth-note triplets may be more difficult to count since they are usually faster.

Another way to count triplets is to feel the three subdivisions while only counting the quarter or eighth notes.

In the next two examples, sixteenth-note triplets and a sextuplet have the same value. They are both counted and played in the same way.

READING

After playing the next five exercise as written, play through them with the two alternate foot patterns showed in Examples A and B, below. These reading exercises can also be practiced using the foot patterns in Chapter 6. The first line of each reading section has the counting written beneath it.

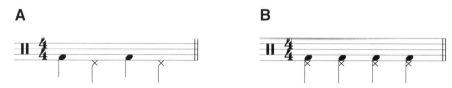

Quarter and Half Notes

TRACK 2
(0:00)

Eighth Notes

TRACK 2
(1:00)

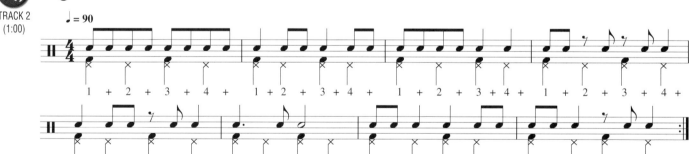

Eighth-Note Triplets

TRACK 2
(1:52)

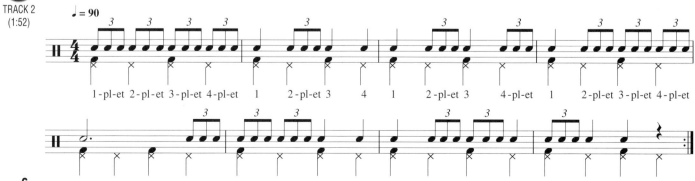

Sixteenth Notes

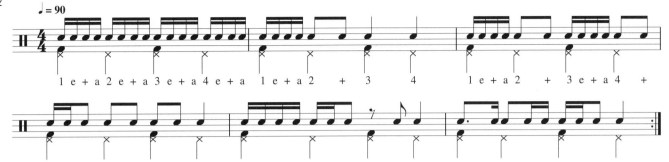

Sixteenth-Note Triplets

EIGHTH-, QUARTER-, AND HALF-NOTE TRIPLETS

The purpose of this next exercise is to practice transitioning between different types of triplets. There is a sticking line written above the exercise. An "R" means a right-hand stroke, and an "L" means a left-hand stroke. In the second and third measures, there is a transition from eighth-note triplets to quarter-note triplets. The larger "Rs" in the sticking of measure 2 set up the quarter-note triplets in measure 3. Drop the left hand out in measure 3 and keep the right hand the same. The same goes for the transition in measures 4 and 5.

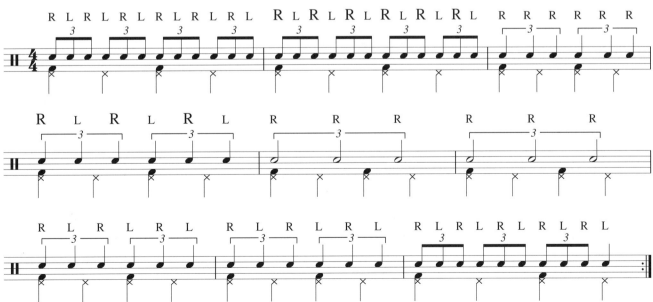

ACCENTS: SIXTEENTH NOTES

An accent is written directly above a note. An accented note is played louder and with more force than non-accented notes. While practicing the following accent patterns, don't forget about the unaccented notes. They need to be clear, consistent, and quieter so the accents stand out. Practice each measure with eighth notes on the hi-hat with foot as well. After learning all the accent patterns on these pages, begin to experiment by moving the accented notes to other parts of the drumset, while keeping the unaccented notes on the snare drum. For example, play the right-hand accents on the low tom and the left-hand accents on the small tom. Accents can also be played on cymbals. Track 4 demonstrates this on the repeats.

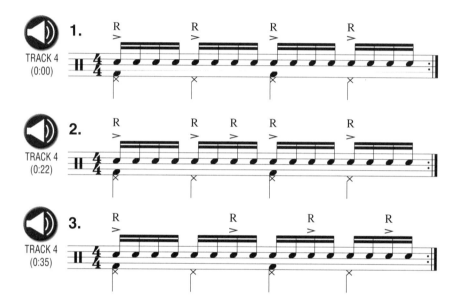

On Track 4, Exercises 6–7 demonstrate some improvisation on the final repeat, playing the accents on cymbals and bass drum, while adding some thirty-second notes in the unaccented snare drum part. Feel free to experiment yourself, hitting the accents in the appropriate rhythms, while freely playing anything between the accented notes.

8.
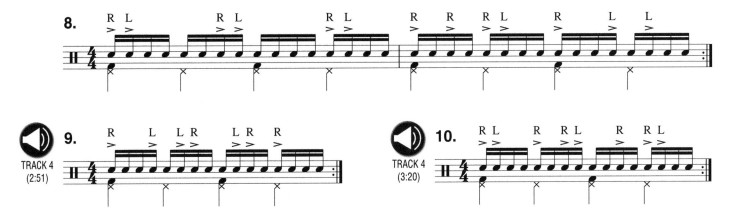

TRACK 4
(2:51)
9.

TRACK 4
(3:20)
10.

ACCENT STICKING: SIXTEENTH NOTES

Exercises 1 and 2 are two examples making use of different stickings with accents. There are single and double strokes together. You may also go back and try experimenting with different stickings in the previous exercises. Track 5 plays the accents on the crash cymbal and bass drum.

TRACK 5
(0:00)
1.

TRACK 5
(0:21)
2.

ACCENTS: EIGHTH-NOTE TRIPLETS

While playing triplets, keep in mind that because of the uneven number of notes in each beat, the sticking changes hands on each quarter-note beat. This is shown in measure one below. After learning the exercise, try moving the accents to the toms or cymbals, with bass drum "kicks."

1.   **2.**

3.   **4.**

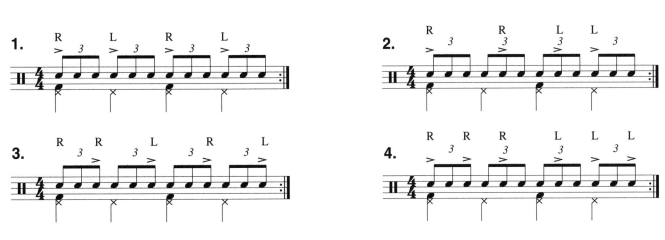

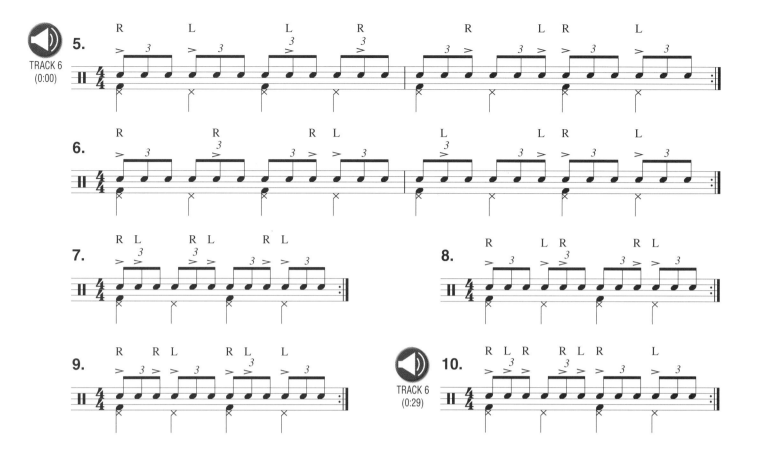

ACCENT READING EXERCISE: EIGHTH-NOTE TRIPLETS

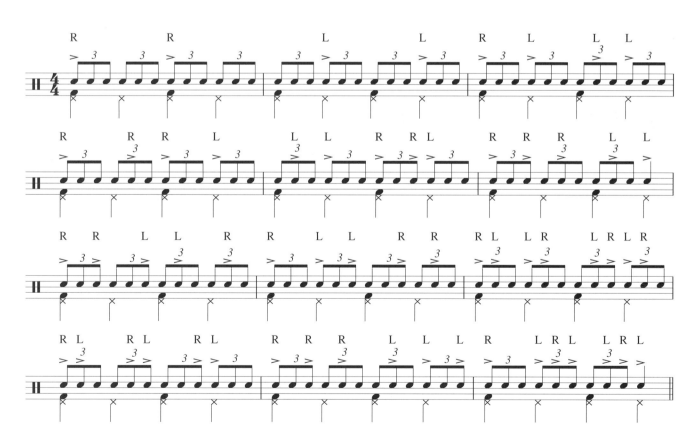

ACCENT STICKING: EIGHTH-NOTE TRIPLETS

The following two exercises are "accent" and "tap" exercises. The same hand plays both the accented and unaccented notes. These are good to practice for stick control and may also be used as warm-up exercises.

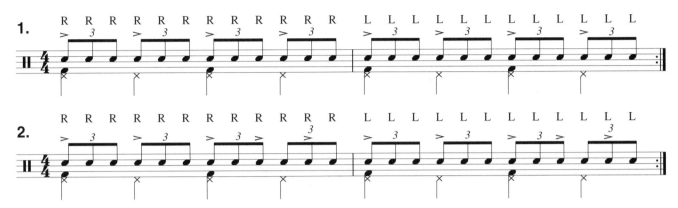

ACCENTS: SIXTEENTH-NOTE TRIPLETS

After playing through this page as it is written, go back and practice each measure with eighth notes on the hi-hat with foot as well. Also move the accents to the toms or cymbals, with bass drum "kicks."

Track 7, the first part combines Exercises 3 and 4.

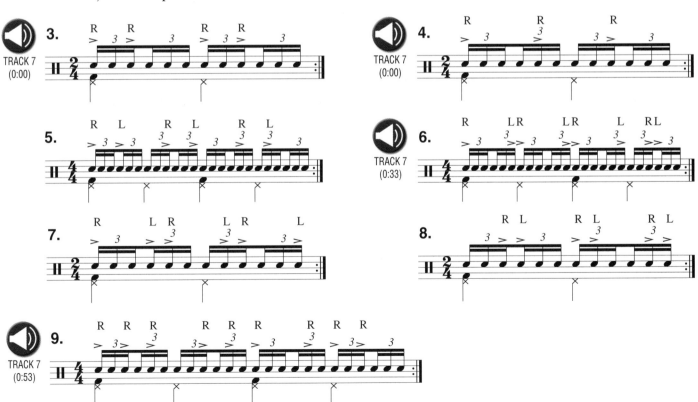

ACCENT READING EXERCISE: SIXTEENTH-NOTE TRIPLETS

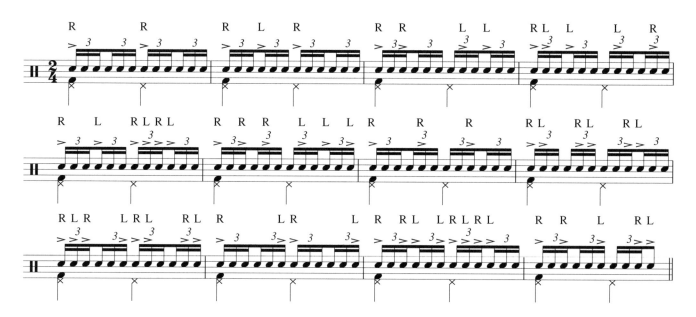

ACCENT STICKING: SIXTEENTH-NOTE TRIPLETS

Here are two examples using different stickings in accent patterns. Instead of all the strokes alternating from hand to hand, the accented notes are single strokes and the unaccented notes are double strokes. You may also experiment with different stickings in the previous exercises.

TRACK 8
(0:00)

TRACK 8
(0:28)

2 RUDIMENTS

This chapter presents the 40 *Percussive Arts Society International Drum Rudiments*. The original *Standard 26 American Drum Rudiments* were assembled in the early 1930s. Later on, fourteen more rudiments were added, and today's list of the 40 International Drum Rudiments was created. The rudiments do not normally appear with a bass drum and hi-hat foot pattern written under them. They have been added here because it is important to learn the rudiments while using the feet. This helps to apply the rudiments to the drumset more effectively, and it helps with timing and independence. The following are a few more topics to cover before moving on to the rudiments.

ROLLS

Rolls are notated with an arcing line (*slur*) that connects two notes together. The note at the end of the roll is called the *release note*. There are two main types of rolls used in drumming. The *multiple bounce roll*, also called a "buzz roll" or a "closed roll," is played by letting each stick bounce as many times as it can naturally. A *double stroke roll* is played by letting the stick bounce twice each time it hits the drum. It is also called an "open roll."

Multiple Bounce Roll

Double Stroke Roll

FLAMS AND DRAGS

A *flam* has a small note, or *grace note*, written to the left of the main note. A flammed note is played using both hands. The primary note is a full stroke and the grace note is a small stroke that lands just before the primary note. Think of a flam as two synchronized divers. One of them is on a thirty-foot high dive and the other is on a ten-foot low dive. If they both jump at the same time, the diver on the low dive will hit the water slightly before the diver on the high dive. In the same way, to play a flam, raise one stick for the primary note and leave the other stick close to the drumhead for the grace note. Let both of the sticks hit the head and the grace note will land just before the primary note.

A *drag* is very similar to a flam except there are two grace notes. They are played as a double stroke with either the right or left hand. Practice flams and drags using both right-hand and left-hand sticking.

Flam   Drag

P.A.S. INTERNATIONAL DRUM RUDIMENTS

I. Roll Rudiments

A. Single Stroke Rudiments

1. Single Stroke Roll*

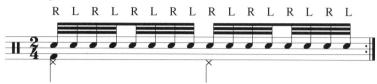

2. Single Stroke Four

3. Single Stroke Seven

B. Multiple Bounce Rudiments

4. Multiple Bounce Roll

5. Triple Stroke Roll

C. Double Stroke Open Roll Rudiments

For section C, the left column shows how the rolls are typically notated. The right column shows how each roll is actually played. Rolls that do not naturally switch hands have the sticking for the opposite hand notated also.

As Written   **As Played**

6. Double Stroke Open Roll*

7. Five Stroke Roll*

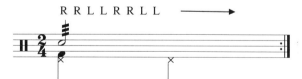

*These rudiments are part of the original Standard 26 American Drum Rudiments.
Reprinted by permission of the Percussive Arts Society, Inc., 32 E. Washington, Suite 1400,
Indianapolis, IN 46204-3516; E-mail: percarts@pas.org; Web: www.pas.org

8. Six Stroke Roll

9. Seven Stroke Roll*

10. Nine Stroke Roll*

11. Ten Stroke Roll*

12. Eleven Stroke Roll*

13. Thirteen Stroke Roll*

14. Fifteen Stroke Roll*

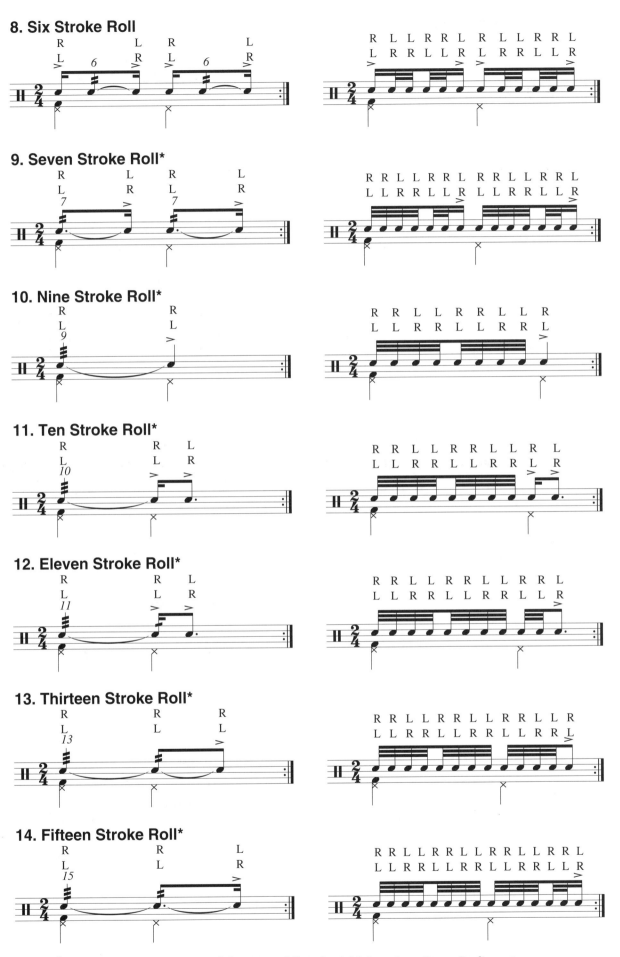

*These rudiments are part of the original Standard 26 American Drum Rudiments.
Reprinted by permission of the Percussive Arts Society, Inc., 32 E. Washington, Suite 1400,
Indianapolis, IN 46204-3516; E-mail: percarts@pas.org; Web: www.pas.org

15. Seventeen Stroke Roll

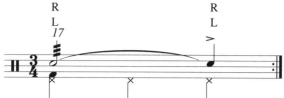

II. Diddle Rudiments

For the double paradiddle and single paradiddle-diddle, there is an optional bass drum note on the "and" of beat 2. These notes are written in parentheses. Playing the extra note creates a "two-against-three" polyrhythm between the feet. Practice these two rudiments both ways.

16. Single Pardiddle*

17. Double Pardiddle*

18. Triple Paradiddle

19. Single Pardiddle-diddle

III. Flam Rudiments

20. Flam*

21. Flam Accent*

22. Flam Tap*

23. Flamacue*

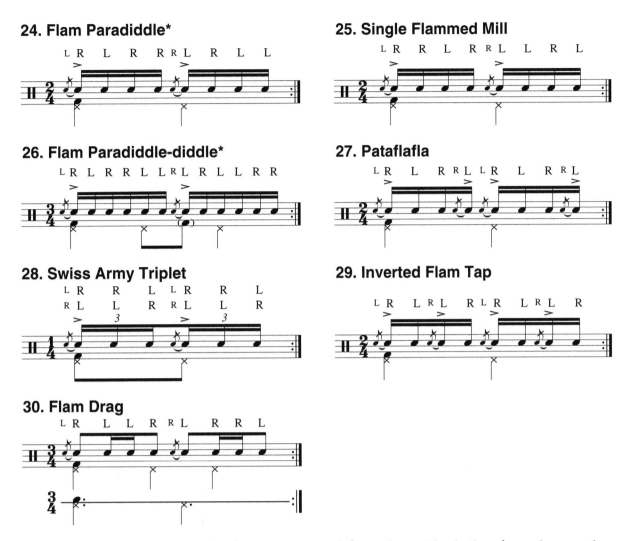

24. Flam Paradiddle*
25. Single Flammed Mill
26. Flam Paradiddle-diddle*
27. Pataflafla
28. Swiss Army Triplet
29. Inverted Flam Tap
30. Flam Drag

There is an alternate foot pattern for *flam accent* and *flam drag*. The hi-hat foot plays on beat 1 and the "and" of beat 2, creating a 6/8 feel. The *flam paradiddle-diddle* has an optional bass drum note in parentheses on the "and" of beat 2. Practice these rudiments as written as well as with the additional foot patterns.

IV. Drag Rudiments

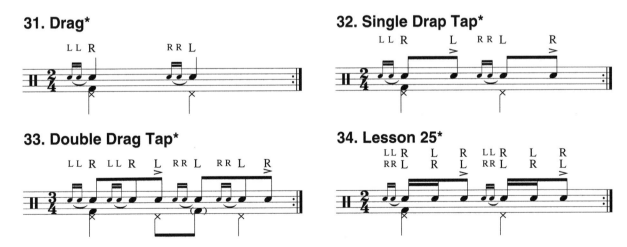

31. Drag*
32. Single Drap Tap*
33. Double Drag Tap*
34. Lesson 25*

*These rudiments are part of the original Standard 26 American Drum Rudiments.
Reprinted by permission of the Percussive Arts Society, Inc., 32 E. Washington, Suite 1400, Indianapolis, IN 46204-3516; E-mail: percarts@pas.org; Web: www.pas.org

35. Single Dragadiddle*

36. Drag Paradiddle #1*

Double drag tap, *drag paradiddle #1*, and *double ratamacue* have an extra bass drum note in parentheses on the "and" of beat 2. This creates a "two-against-three" polyrhythm between the feet.

37. Drag Paradiddle #2*

38. Single Ratamacue*

39. Double Ratamacue*

40. Triple Ratamacue*

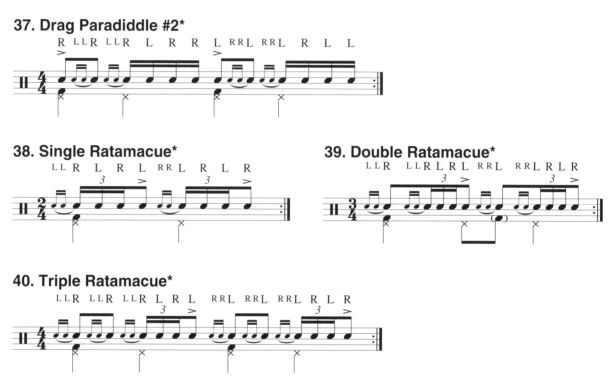

Mommy Daddy Rolls

The *double stroke open roll* is a very important and versatile rudiment. When learning a new rudiment, having a word or phrase to say which matches the beats of the rudiment is a great way to practice. For the double stroke roll, "mommy-daddy-mommy-daddy" works well. Each stroke has a matching syllable. This is shown in the next example. The rest of this section shows how to play double strokes in different rhythms.

*These rudiments are part of the original Standard 26 American Drum Rudiments.
Reprinted by permission of the Percussive Arts Society, Inc., 32 E. Washington, Suite 1400,
Indianapolis, IN 46204-3516; E-mail: percarts@pas.org; Web: www.pas.org

Track 9 plays Exercises 1–4 continuously, and then repeats, playing the right-hand strokes on the floor tom.

TRACK 9
Ex. 1–4

1. Eighth Notes

2. Eighth-Note Triplets

3. Sixteenth Notes

4. Sixteenth-Note Triplets

FIVE, SIX, SEVEN, AND NINE STROKE ROLLS

This exercise starts with five stroke rolls, increases to nine stroke rolls, and then back down to five stroke rolls. Halfway through this exercise, it changes from right-hand lead rolls to left-hand lead rolls.

TRACK 10

FIVE STROKE ROLL VARIATIONS

Here are three different ways of playing five stroke rolls in a 4/4 measure. Exercise 1 starts with a roll at the beginning of the measure. Exercise 2 has the rolls starting on the "and" of beat one, and in Exercise 3, the rolls begin on the "e" of beat one. These are all good variations to use in fills and solos.

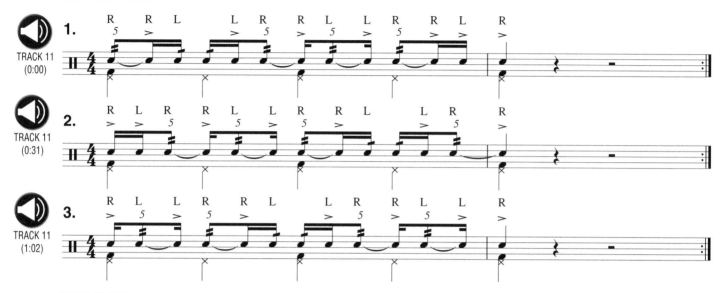

TRACK 11 (0:00) **1.**

TRACK 11 (0:31) **2.**

TRACK 11 (1:02) **3.**

TRAIN

His teacher, British jazz drummer, Phil Seamen, originally taught this next exercise to Ginger Baker. The story goes that while riding on a British rail train, Phil wrote this exercise to mimic the rhythm of the train clacking over the tracks, and the wheels skipping where the track sections connected. It is a good exercise for practicing double strokes as well as for endurance. Learn it at a slow tempo first and gradually speed it up.

Once this exercise has been learned, try experimenting with it. Change the sticking, or change what the feet play. For example, play all the sticking single stroked or as paradiddles. Also, try some different patterns with the feet. One alternative foot pattern would be to play quarter notes on the bass drum, and eighth notes on the hi-hat with foot.

PARADIDDLES

Another important rudiment is the paradiddle. It is a combination of two single strokes and one double stroke. Then the pattern repeats itself, starting with the opposite hand. The measure below shows how the word "paradiddle" mimics the rhythm of the rudiment. While learning this rudiment, say the words out loud with each stroke. This helps the brain connect with the hands and it aids in promoting better coordination. Practice the rest of the page to see how paradiddles fit into different types of notes.

1. Eighth Notes

2. Eighth-Note Triplets

3. Sixteenth Notes

4. Sixteenth-Note Triplets

MOMMY DADDY PARADIDDLES

The *mommy daddy paradiddle* is a combination of the double stroke roll and the paradiddle.

1. Eighth Notes

2. Sixteenth Notes

THE FOUR PARADIDDLES

There are four variations of the paradiddle. The first one has already been covered. The other three start the paradiddle from different points to create new sticking patterns. Exercise 2 has the diddle on the inside of the rhythm. Exercise 3 starts with the diddle, and in Exercise 4, the diddles are at the beginning and the end of the pattern, like bookends. The accents follow the paradiddle, so they are different in each measure. Repeat these exercises until they can be comfortably played at any tempo.

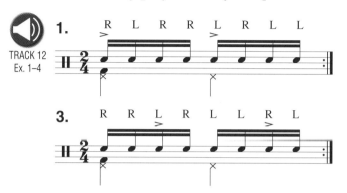

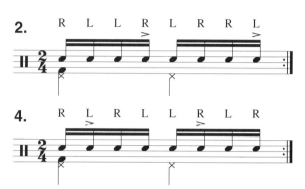

TRACK 12
Ex. 1–4

DOUBLE PARADIDDLES

The *double paradiddle* is similar to the paradiddle, except it has two extra single strokes at the beginning. These extra strokes make the double paradiddle take up three beats. For this reason, they fit nicely into 3/4 or 6/8, as well as triplets.

The following are the syllables for the double paradiddle and examples of how it can be used in different rhythms. The double paradiddles in this section have two accents.

dou - ble pa - ra - did - dle dou - ble pa - ra - did - dle

TRACK 13
Ex. 1–4

1. Eighth Notes*

2. Eighth-Note Triplets

3. Sixteenth Notes*

*For double paradiddles in eighth notes and sixteenth notes, the time signature is 3/4, but the foot pattern is played as if it were in 2/4. The bass drum lands on beats 1 and 3 in the first measure, and on beat 2 in the second measure, while the hi-hat with foot plays quarter notes.

4. Sixteenth-Note Triplets

RUDIMENTS IN PARADIDDLE FORM

Next is an additional idea for practicing rudiments. Try playing the rudiments in paradiddle form. This means that the rudiment changes hands in the form of a paradiddle: R-L-R-R-L-R-L-L. Each quarter note in the measure is the next stroke of the paradiddle, so it takes two measures to complete the pattern. This is shown in the following example.

Exercises 1 and 2 are examples of rudiments being played in paradiddle form.

1. Six Stroke Roll

TRACK 14
(0:00)

2. Flam Accent

TRACK 14
(0:24)

This idea also works with the following rudiments: single stroke four, five stroke roll, seven stroke roll, flam drags, single flammed mill, pataflafla, Swiss army triplets, and lesson 25.

Exercise 3 uses a different pattern for the paradiddle form. In this line the paradiddle form follows the accents instead of the quarter note. The bigger letters in the sticking line show the paradiddle form. The sticking pattern is two paradiddles and a double paradiddle. The time signature is 7/4, which means there are seven quarter notes in the measure, and the quarter note gets the beat.

3. Paradiddles and Double Paradiddles

TRACK 14
(0:58)

3 ROCK BEATS AND FILLS

The rock beats in this chapter are broken into four different parts: Eighth Notes on the Bass Drum, Eighth Notes on the Snare Drum, Sixteenth Notes on the Snare Drum, and Sixteenth Notes on the Bass Drum. Work through each section because they build on each other. There are also four Melody Line Reading Exercises in this chapter. Melody line exercises are good for sight reading and coordination. Play though the melody lines with all the beats listed. The melody lines throughout the book can be practiced as left-hand snare lines against cymbal patterns, or as reading exercises over the foot patterns in Chapter 6.

The last section of this chapter is Rock Fills. Four-measure phrases are presented in which the fills may be inserted. This helps the drummer develop the skill of being able to play a fill and then get right back into a beat without a loss of continuity.

Hi-Hat with Foot Patterns

The beats in this chapter are written with quarter notes on the hi-hat with foot. Also play through the beats with the hi-hat foot playing eighth notes and upbeat eighth notes as in the following patterns.

Eighth Notes

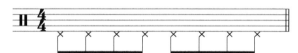

Upbeat Eighth Notes

Cymbal Line Patterns

The cymbal line for any of the rock beats can also be changed. Try playing quarter notes or upbeat eighth notes. After learning the beats in this chapter as written, experiment with different hi-hat foot and cymbal line combinations. For example, play quarter notes on the cymbal line with eighth notes on the hi-hat with foot.

Quarter Notes

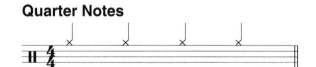

Upbeat Eighth Notes

ROCK BEATS: EIGHTH NOTES ON BASS DRUM

TRACK 15
Ex. 1–10

Two-Measure Phrases

Four-Measure Phrases

TRACK 16
Ex. 1, 2

1.

2.

Eight-Measure Phrase

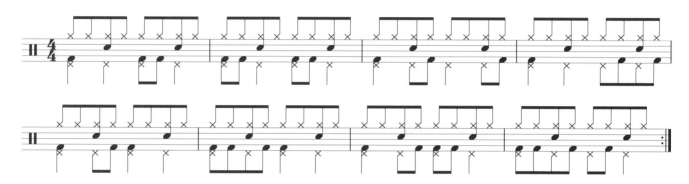

MELODY LINE READING

This section includes a bass drum melody line, which is to be played against the five cymbal/snare patterns. The first three patterns have the same hand rhythm with different hi-hat foot rhythms: quarter notes, eighth notes, and upbeat eighth notes. Patterns 4 and 5 have different cymbal rhythms.

Cymbal/Snare Patterns

Bass Drum Melody Line

ROCK BEATS: EIGHTH NOTES ON SNARE DRUM

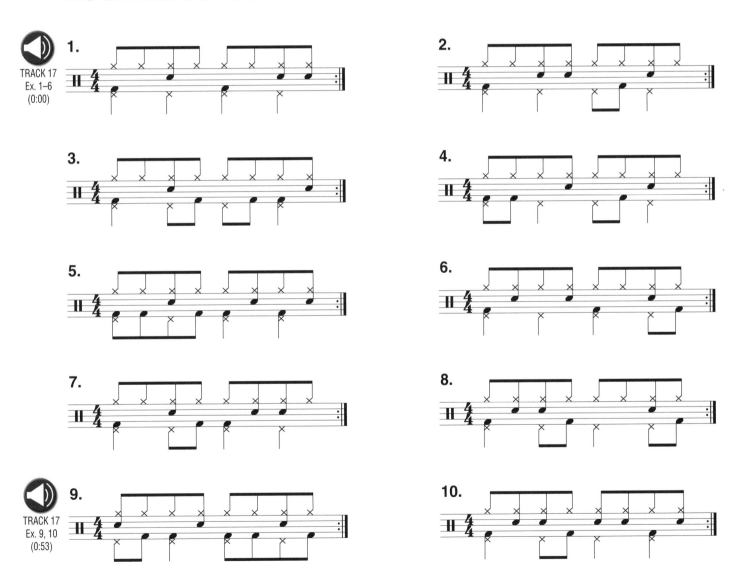

TRACK 17
Ex. 1–6
(0:00)

TRACK 17
Ex. 9, 10
(0:53)

Two-Measure Phrases

1.

2.

3.

4.

Four-Measure Phrases

1.

2.

Eight-Measure Phrase

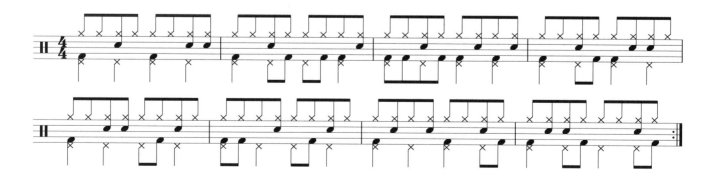

MELODY LINE READING

This section includes a snare drum melody line, which is to be played against the four cymbal/bass drum patterns. The first two patterns have the same hand rhythm with different hi-hat foot and bass drum rhythms. Patterns 3 and 4 have different cymbal rhythms, but the same foot rhythms.

Cymbal/Bass Drum/Hi-Hat Foot Patterns

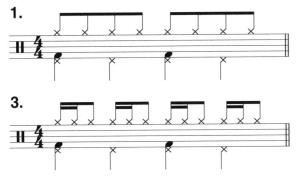

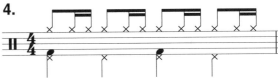

Snare Drum Melody Line

ROCK BEATS: SIXTEENTH NOTES ON SNARE DRUM

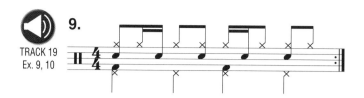

Two-Measure Phrases

Four-Measure Phrases

Eight-Measure Phrase

MELODY LINE READING

This section shows a snare drum melody line, which is to be played against the four cymbal/bass drum/hi-hat foot patterns below. The first two patterns have eighth notes on the cymbal with different foot rhythms. Patterns 3 and 4 have the same foot pattern (as each other), but with different sixteenth-note cymbal rhythms.

Cymbal/Bass Drum Patterns

Snare Drum Melody Line

ROCK BEATS: SIXTEENTH NOTES ON BASS DRUM

Play each exercise four times.

Two-Measure Phrases

Four-Measure Phrases

Eight-Measure Phrase

MELODY LINE READING

This section presents a bass drum melody line, which is to be played against the five cymbal/snare drum patterns below. The first three patterns have eighth notes on the cymbal with different foot rhythms. Patterns 4 and 5 have the same foot rhythm (as each other), but with different sixteenth-note cymbal rhythms.

Cymbal/Snare Drum Patterns

1.

2.

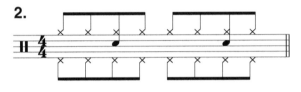

3.

4.

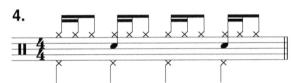

5.

Bass Drum Melody Line

MORE ROCK BEATS

This section presents six different categories of rock beats:

1. Combination Beats
2. Paradiddles on Drumset
3. Drags in Beats
4. Rock Beats in 6/8
5. Rock Beats in 3/4
6. Rock Beats with Sixteenth Notes on Cymbal

Combination Beats

The following beats combine sixteenth notes on the bass drum and snare drum. Try creating other combinations from the beats in this chapter. Each exercise on the track is played four times.

TRACK 22
Ex. 1, 5, 6

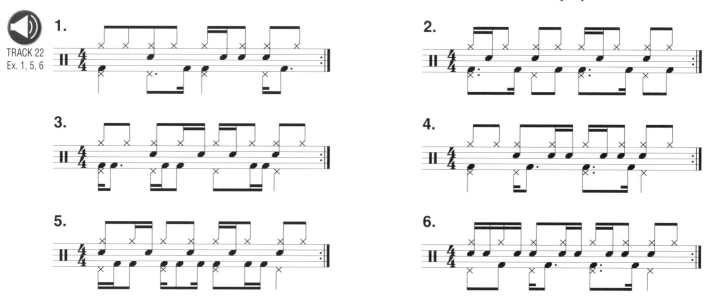

Paradiddles on Drumset

The following example shows three different ways of applying the paradiddle to a drumset beat. Track 23 plays all three examples continuously.

TRACK 23
Ex. 1–3

34

Drags in Beats

Drags are a great way to add variety to beats or fills. Start out by playing the single drag tap (Exercise 1). Notice that the sticking has been changed (from how it was presented in Chapter 2) so that all the eighth notes are played with the right hand and all the drags are played with the left hand. Exercise 2 moves the right hand to the cymbal, keeps the left-hand drags on the snare, and adds the feet. Exercise 3 is the full transition of the single drag tap to a rock beat. The drags on beats 2 and 4 are now normal snare hits, and the bass drum is only played on beats 1 and 3.

TRACK 24
Ex. 1–6

The next example uses the double drag tap. Here, there is a second tap added to it, making it the "double drag tap tap." Exercise 4 shows the new sticking for the rudiment. Exercise 5 moves the right hand to the cymbal, keeps the left-hand drags on the snare, and adds the feet. The last example sees the addition of snare hit on beats 2 and 4 to create a rock beat using the double drag tap.

On Track 24, Exercise 6 is played with the hi-hat the first time, and the ride cymbal on the repeat. Attempt your own variations of this type on all of the examples.

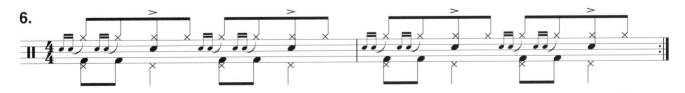

Rock Beats in 6/8

In 6/8 time, the bottom number, "8," means that the eighth note gets the count (or the feel), and the top number, "6," means there are six eighth notes in each measure. However, in 6/8, the beat is often felt "in two," or one beat for every three eighth notes (or one beat for each dotted quarter note). On Track 25, the click will sound on the dotted quarter-note beat (two beats per measure), but the count off will use the six eighth notes.

This section features 6/8 drum beats ranging from basic to advanced. There are two different hi-hat foot patterns to use with these beats. In Exercise 1, the left foot plays on beats 1, 3, and 5, or every other eighth note. This feels as if the left foot is playing in 3/4 not 6/8. Think of the counting like this: 1 2 - 3 4 - 5 6. In Exercise 2, the left foot plays on beats 1 and 4, or every three eighth notes. This creates a three-feel like in a waltz: 1 2 3 - 4 5 6. The beats in this section use the hi-hat pattern from Exercise 1. After learning these exercises as written, practice all the beats with the hi-hat foot pattern from Exercise 2.

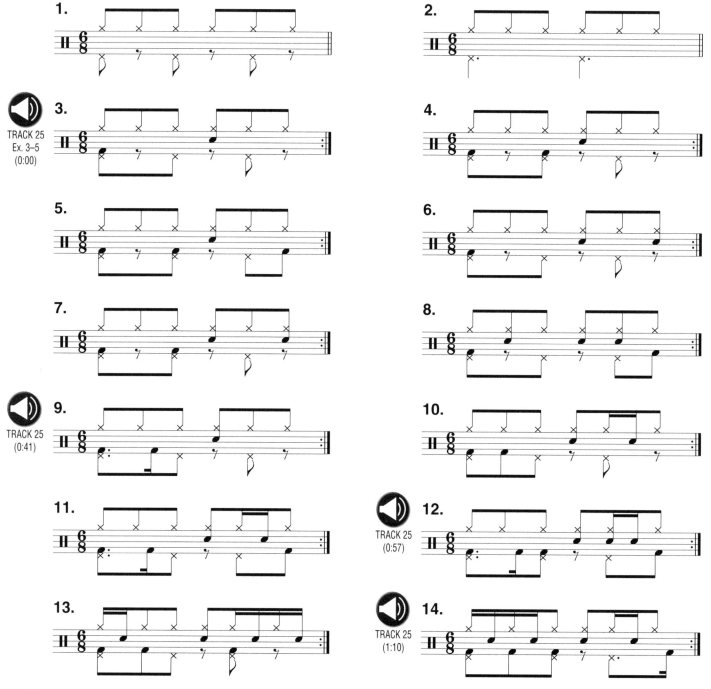

TRACK 25
Ex. 3–5
(0:00)

TRACK 25
(0:41)

TRACK 25
(0:57)

TRACK 25
(1:10)

Rock Beats in 3/4

Playing in 3/4 is similar to 6/8 because both have six eighth notes in each measure. They are just phrased or accented differently. The polyrhythms "two against three" (2:3), and "three against four" (3:4), both fit in one measure of 3/4. The foot pattern in Exercises 1 and 4 is 2:3. In Exercises 5, 7, 8, and 10, the feet are playing the polyrhythm 3:4. For fill ideas in both 3/4 and 6/8, use the Reading and Accent exercises from the 3:4 Foot Pattern in Chapter 6.

Rock Beats with Sixteenth Notes on Cymbal

For sixteenth-note rock beats there are two ways the cymbal part can be played. The first uses both hands on the hi-hat cymbal, with the right hand playing the snare drum on beats 2 and 4 (these are the large "R"s in Exercise 1). The left hand will also play the snare in some measures. Exercise 2 shows the right hand playing all the cymbal notes and the left hand playing all the snare notes. This option is good to use for slower tempos. Keep the hi-hat closed when using the Exercise 1 cymbal pattern, and play eighth notes with the hi-hat foot for Exercise 2. Go back through this chapter and practice all the beats with sixteenth notes on the cymbal.

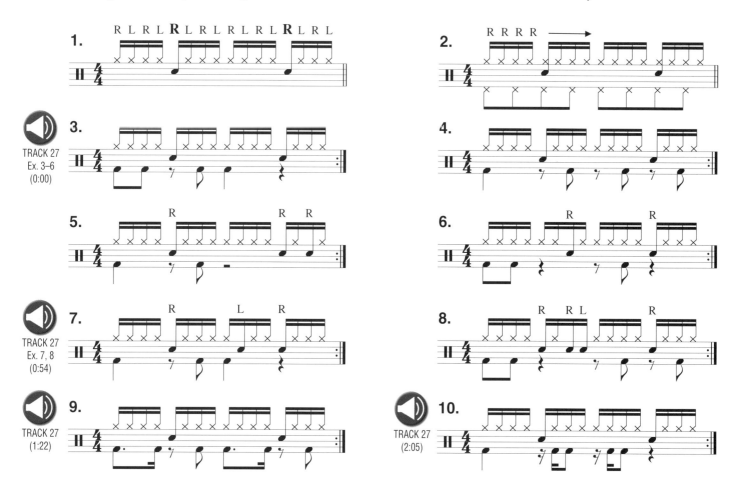

TRACK 27
Ex. 3–6
(0:00)

TRACK 27
Ex. 7, 8
(0:54)

TRACK 27
(1:22)

TRACK 27
(2:05)

ROCK FILLS

In this next section, fills will be presented in nine different categories:

1. Sixteenth-Note Fills
2. Sixteenth-Note Triplets Fills
3. Sixteenth-Note Crashes
4. Sixteenth-Note Triplet Crashes
5. Half-Measure Fills
6. Flams
7. Fills in Beats
8. Hand-to-Foot Singles
9. Hand-to-Foot Doubles

Each category begins with a four-measure phrase containing two blank measures in which the fills are to be inserted. This is good practice for playing a fill and getting right back into the beat. Fills are a personal and expressive part of drumming. These exercises should be learned and then personalized with accents, toms, and flams.

Sixteenth-Note Fills

This category features different combinations of sixteenth-note rhythms. The fills are notated with quarter notes on the hi-hat with foot. Also practice these with eighth notes on the hi-hat foot.

Phrase

TRACK 28
Phrase,
Ex. 3, 7

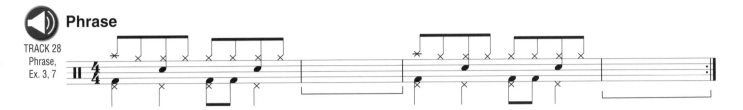

Insert a fill from below in the blank measures above.

1.

2.

3.

Try putting the rudiment Lesson 25 in this fill.

4.

5.
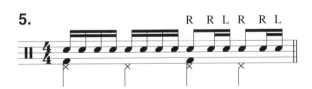

6.

7.

8.

Sixteenth-Note Triplets Fills

After learning the following fills, try making new combinations of sixteenth notes and sixteenth-note triplets. Also try incorporating the rhythms from the previous category. The hi-hat foot is notated in quarter notes. Practice these exercises with eighth notes on the hi-hat foot as well.

Phrase

TRACK 29
Phrase,
Ex. 2-4, 6

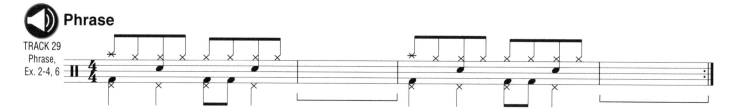

Insert a fill from below in the blank measures above.

1.

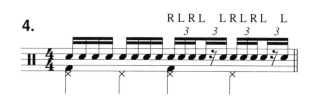

2.

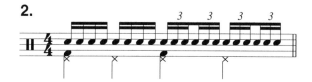

3.

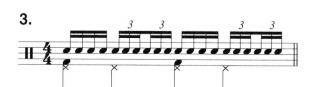

4.

5.

6.

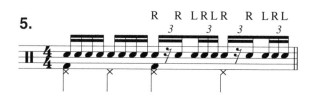

Sixteenth-Note Crashes

The sticking for the crash cymbals are written above each fill. Also play these exercises with eighth notes on the hi-hat with foot.

Phrase

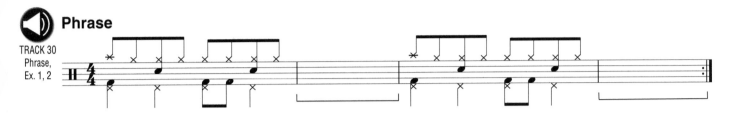

Insert a fill from below in the blank measures above.

1.

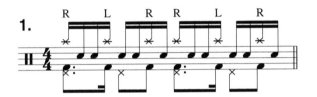

2.

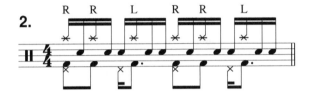

3.

4.

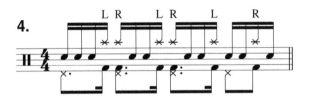

5.

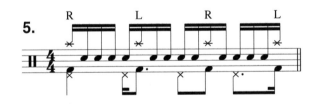

6.

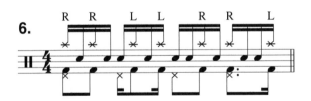

7.

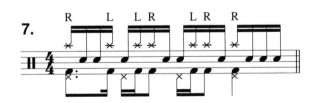

8.

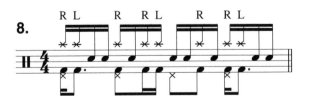

Sixteenth-Note Triplet Crashes

The sticking patterns for the crash cymbals are written above each fill. Exercise 3 has two different sticking options: the first is alternating single strokes, with all the crashes on the right hand; the second uses paradiddles and causes the crashes to switch hands back and forth.

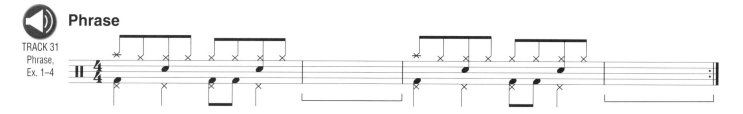

Phrase

TRACK 31
Phrase,
Ex. 1–4

Insert a fill from below in the blank measures above.

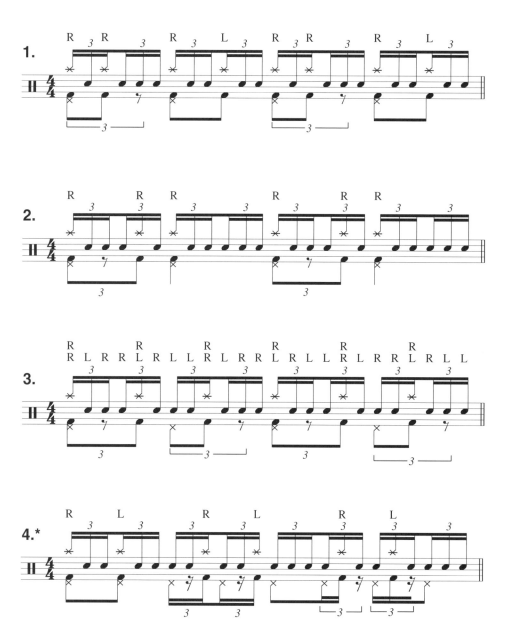

*Exercise 4 has eighth notes on the hi-hat with foot. Also play Exercises 1–3 with
eighth notes on the hi-hat with foot.

Half-Measure Fills

In this category, fills begin on beat 3 of each measure, making the fills only half a measure in length.

Phrase

TRACK 32
Phrase,
Ex. 5–7

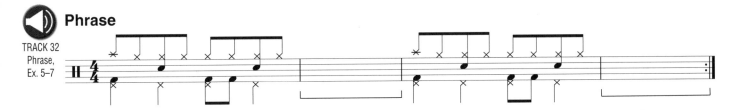

Insert a fill from below in the blank measures above.

1. **2.**

Exercises 3 and 4 have two different sticking patterns. The top sticking line is alternating single strokes, and the bottom sticking line uses single and double strokes.

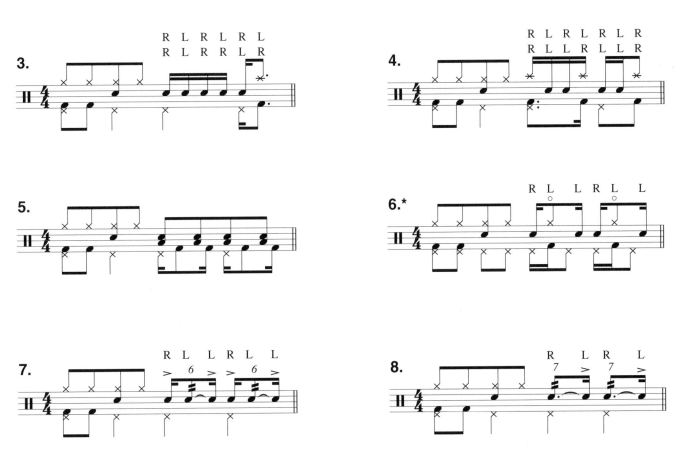

*Exercise 6 has eighth notes on the hi-hat with foot instead of quarter notes. This is so the hi-hat closes right after it is played during the fill. Also practice the rest of the exercises with eighth notes on the hi-hat with foot.

Flams

It is important to be comfortable with both right- and left-handed flams. There are times when left-handed flams are more useful than right-handed flams. When playing down the toms, use left-handed flams because the right hand will be playing the grace note, moving down the set in front of the left hand (this would be the opposite for a left-handed drumset configuration). Beat 4 in Exercise 2 uses a left-handed single-flammed mill. This works well because it sets up the right-hand crash on the downbeat of the next measure.

Phrase

TRACK 33
Phrase,
Ex. 1, 2, 4,
6, 7

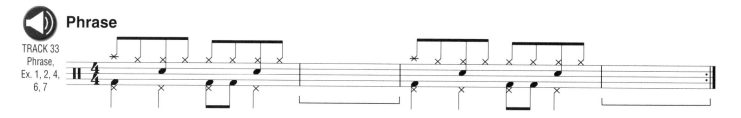

Insert a fill from below in the blank measures above.

1.

2.

3.

4.

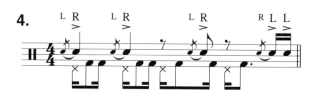

5.

6.

7.

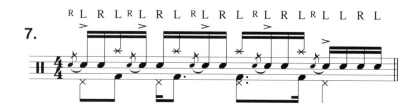

Fills in Beats

These fills keep the feel of a beat going throughout the measure. Exercises 4, 5, 6, 7, and 8 have the bass drum notes connected (by stems) up to the hands during the triplet rhythms to help make them easier to read.

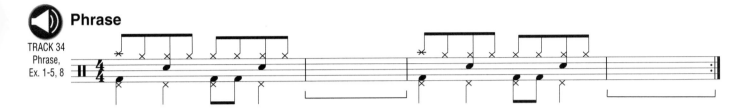

Phrase

TRACK 34
Phrase,
Ex. 1-5, 8

Insert a fill from below in the blank measures above.

*Exercises 2, 5, and 6 have the hi-hat with foot playing eighth notes instead of quarter notes.
When inserting these fills in the phrase, play eighth notes with the hi-hat foot through all
four measures.

Hand-to-Foot Singles

The fills in this category follow a three-note pattern: hand-hand-foot. The speed of the pattern depends on what type of note is being played. The three-note pattern is played in sixteenth notes, sixteenth-note triplets, and triplet triplets (beats 3 and 4 of Exercise 6).

There are different stickings for most of the fills. The hands can either be played alternating: R-L-R-L, or hand-to-hand: R-L-L-R. The third option is in Exercise 5, where some of the notes are played together as double hits on snare drum and floor tom.

All the fills in this category have the bass drum notes connected up to the hand notes. In Exercises 4 and 6, the downbeat bass drum note in the Phrase comes very quickly after the last bass drum note in the fill. If using a double bass drum (or double-bass drum pedal), the downbeat bass drum note in the Phrase can be played with the left foot. This may be easier than playing a double stroke with the right foot, which you would have to do if you only have one bass drum.

Also, practice these fills with eighth notes on the hi-hat with foot.

Phrase

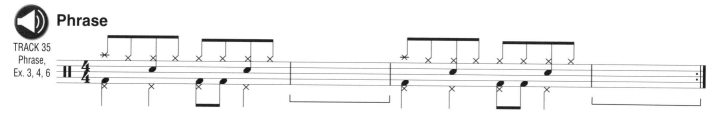

Insert a fill from below in the blank measures above.

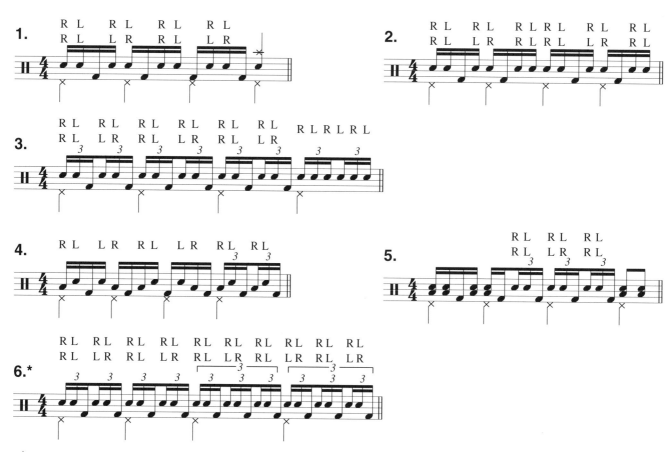

*The triplet rhythms on beats 3 and 4 of Exercise 6 are not as confusing as they may look. The right hand plays eighth-note triplets and then the left hand and bass drum fit in between. Listen to Track 35 carefully to help get the feel of this rhythm. This track first plays the fill as written, and then plays it with the "triplet-triplet" (notated on beats 3 and 4) on beats 1 and 2, and the sixteenth-note triplets on beats 3 and 4.

Hand-to-Foot Doubles

These fills follow the same idea as in "Hand-to-Foot Singles," except the bass drum is now playing two notes instead of one. There are alternate stickings for some of the fills. Once they have been learned as written, try moving the hands around to different drums. Also note that the Phrase has a slightly different rhythm in the bass drum. You may play this Phrase, or the Phrase from the previous categories, or make up your own phrase in which to insert the fills. Practice these exercises with eighth notes on the hi-hat with foot as well.

Phrase

TRACK 36
Phrase,
Ex. 1, 3

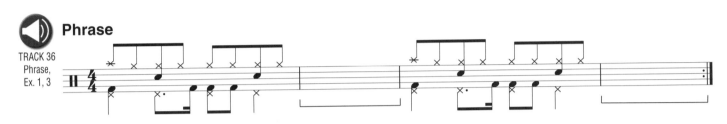

Insert a fill from below in the blank measures above.

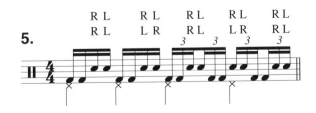

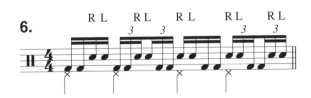

4 SHUFFLE AND JAZZ

This chapter presents three basic shuffle/jazz cymbal patterns: shuffle, jazz and Afro-Cuban. They are similar to one another because they all have a triplet feel.

Shuffle

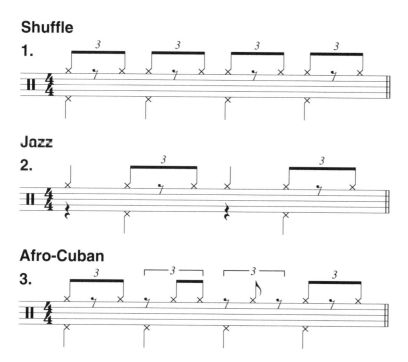

Jazz

Afro-Cuban

All of the exercises in this chapter are written with the shuffle cymbal pattern. After learning the exercises as written, go back and practice them with the jazz and Afro-Cuban cymbal patterns. The hi-hat foot plays quarter notes for the shuffle and Afro-Cuban patterns. In the jazz cymbal pattern, the hi-hat foot only plays on beats 2 and 4.

INDEPENDENCE EXERCISES

This next section includes exercises that develop and improve independence while playing the cymbal patterns. After learning the exercises as written, go back and play them with the jazz and Afro-Cuban cymbal patterns.

The following Exercise shows the basic shuffle pattern with the snare and bass drum added. Practice this first to get comfortable with it, as it is the foundation for the exercises that follow.

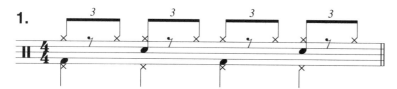

In the next exercises, learn them one measure at a time, and then put them together.

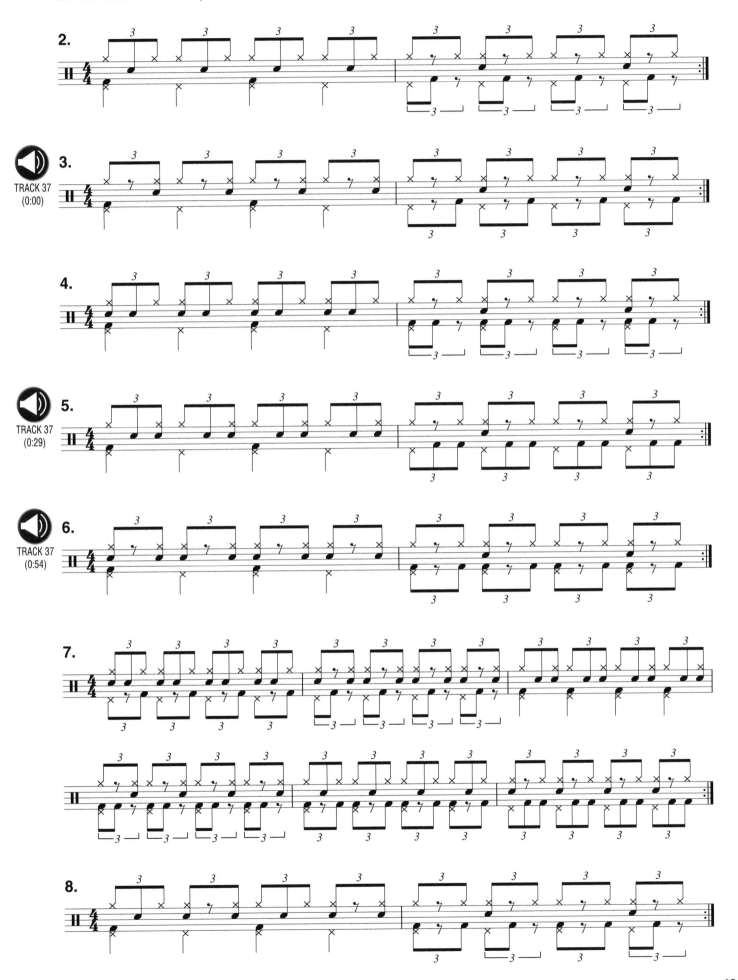

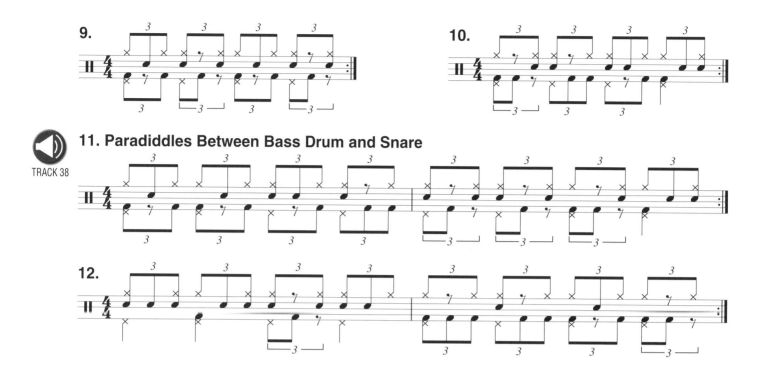

9.   **10.**

11. Paradiddles Between Bass Drum and Snare

12.

TWO-MEASURE PHRASES

Standard Phrases

Exercises 1–3 include some additional two-measure phrases. Practice them with the jazz and Afro-Cuban cymbal patterns as well. Use the rhythms from the previous section to create other two-measure phrases.

1.

2.

3.

Mirror Phrases

In Exercises 4–6, the hand patterns mirror each other in that the hands invert from the first measure of the phrase to the second measure. For example, in the first measure of Exercise 5, the right hand plays the shuffle cymbal pattern while the snare plays the Afro-Cuban pattern. In the second measure, the right hand plays the Afro-Cuban pattern and the shuffle pattern moves to the left hand on the snare.

4.

5.

TRACK 39
(0:25)

6.

ADDITIONAL JAZZ AND SHUFFLE BEATS

The following include some additional important jazz and shuffle beats. For Exercises 1 and 6 try playing different bass drum patterns.

TRACK 40
(0:00)

1. Jazz Rock

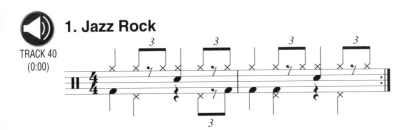

2. Jazz Waltz A

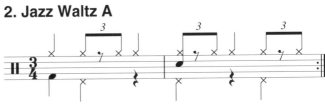

TRACK 40
(0:22)

3. Jazz Waltz B

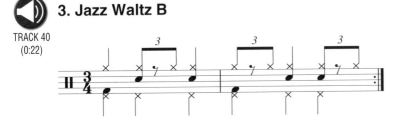

4. Jazz Latin with 2-3 Rhumba Clave on the Snare

When repeating the jazz Latin beat, leave out the down-beat bass drum note.

5. Half-Time Shuffle A

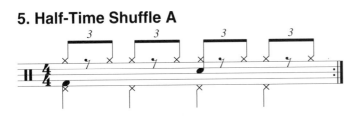

TRACK 40
(0:40)

6. Half-Time Shuffle B

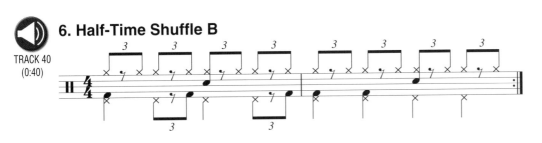

SHUFFLE AND JAZZ FILLS

This page has several fills for shuffle and jazz beats. Practice them using the four-measure phrase shown. Also practice this page with the jazz and Afro-Cuban cymbal patterns. These eighth-note triplet fills can also be used when playing rock.

Phrase

TRACK 41
Phrase,
Ex. 2, 3, 5, 7

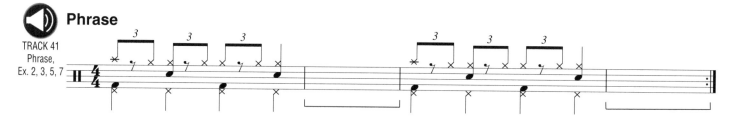

Insert a fill from below in the blank measures above.

1.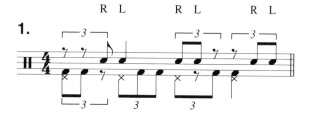

2.

3.

4.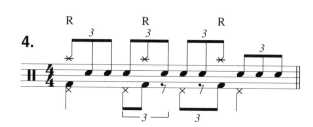

5.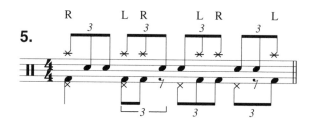

6.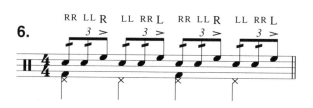

7.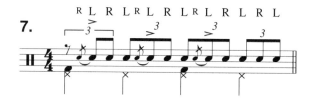

8.

5 DOUBLE BASS DRUM

There are several topics to cover before we get into the exercises. The first is "right-foot versus left-foot lead." As with the hands, the feet can lead with either the right or the left. It is safe to say that the majority of right-handed drummers also play right-foot lead for double bass drum, but there are drummers that use left-foot lead also. This book does not intend to convert any one drummer's style of playing, but only to introduce new concepts to explore. There are both right-foot and left-foot lead exercises in this chapter.

The following example shows what right-foot and left-foot lead look like when notated.

right foot starting rhythm

left foot starting rhythm

The second topic to cover is "pedal bridging." This is a technique in which the left foot plays the hi-hat pedal and the second bass drum pedal at the same time. Many bass drum pedals have adjustable foot boards, and most hi-hat stands are equipped with either a swiveling tripod or only have two legs. With these features, the footboards of the hi-hat pedal and the bass drum pedal can be positioned close enough together that both pedals can be played with one foot. For players that have two separate bass drums, a bracket clamp is available that will attach the hi-hat stand to the rim of the bass drum. This also allows the two pedals to be close to each other.

Here is a notated example of what pedal bridging looks like when written out:

left foot playing both the bass drum and hi-hat pedals

Pedal bridging while playing left-foot lead allows the hi-hat to continue being played during double bass drum beats. This is a way to use left-foot coordination to play rhythms otherwise not possible. Pedal bridging can be used on any exercise in this book.

DOUBLE BASS DRUM BEATS

All of the beats in this section are notated with right-foot lead on the bass drums.

CYMBAL PATTERNS OVER SIXTEENTH-NOTE DOUBLE BASS DRUM

All of the exercises on this page have straight sixteenth notes on the bass drums. Note the variety of different cymbal and snare patterns.

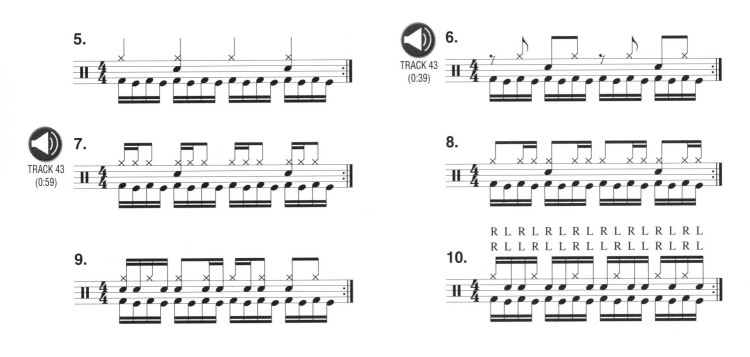

TWO-MEASURE DOUBLE BASS DRUM PHRASES

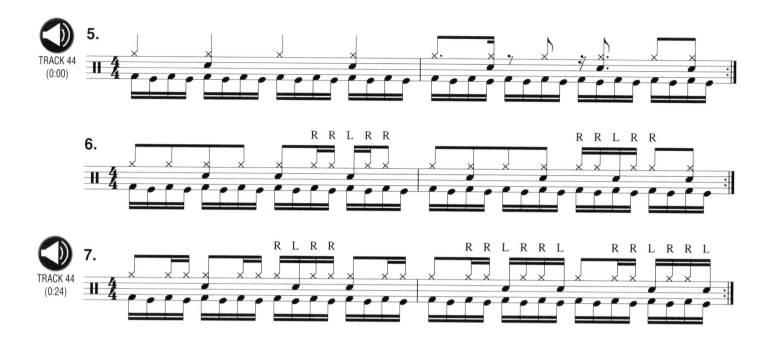

PEDAL BRIDGING: QUARTER NOTES

This section serves as an introduction to pedal bridging, defined earlier in this chapter. As shown in Exercise 1, the left foot plays regular quarter notes. Looking at the remaining exercises, you'll see the left foot continues, playing quarter notes, even while the right foot plays different rhythms. Sometimes the right foot will line up with the left foot, and other times the right foot will land in between left-foot quarter notes. Exercise 1 also shows the notation that is used when both pedals are played together.

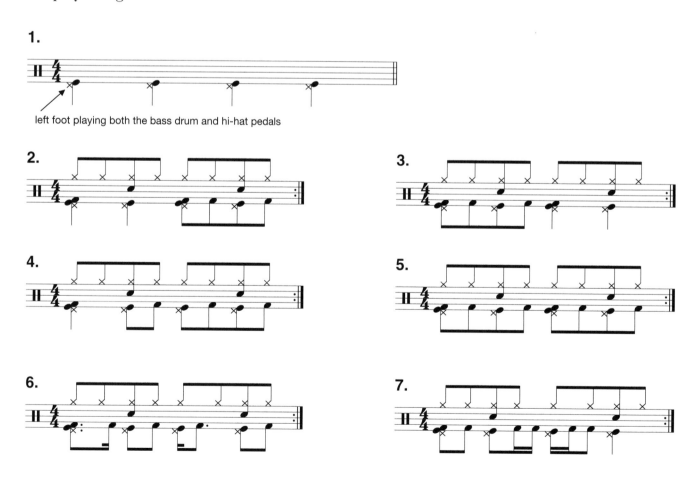

left foot playing both the bass drum and hi-hat pedals

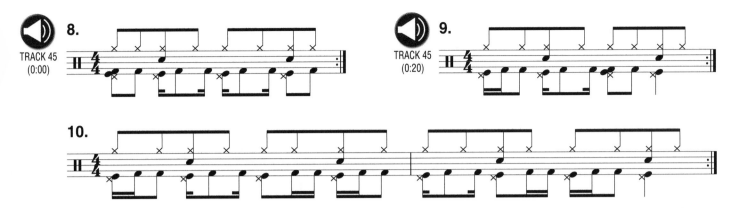

8. TRACK 45 (0:00)   **9.** TRACK 45 (0:20)

10.

PEDAL BRIDGING: EIGHTH NOTES

In this next section, the left foot plays regular eighth notes throughout each beat. The right foot fills in the sixteenth notes between the left-foot eighth notes. This results in the exercises using a left-foot lead on the bass drums. Exercises 2 and 3 have the "footing" ("sticking," for feet) written below the bass drum notes.

1.

left foot playing both the bass drum and hi-hat pedals

2. TRACK 46 (0:00)

L R L L L L R L L L R L L L R

3.

L R L R L L L R L R L L L R L

4.   **5.**

6. TRACK 46 (0:28)   **7.**

8.   **9.**

10.   **11.**

SIXTEENTH-NOTE TRIPLETS ON DOUBLE BASS DRUM

1.

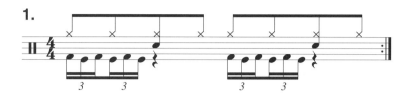

On Track 47, the hi-hat plays a variation on what is notated by adding some sixteenth notes.

TRACK 47
(0:00)

2.

3.

TRACK 47
(0:23)

4.

5.

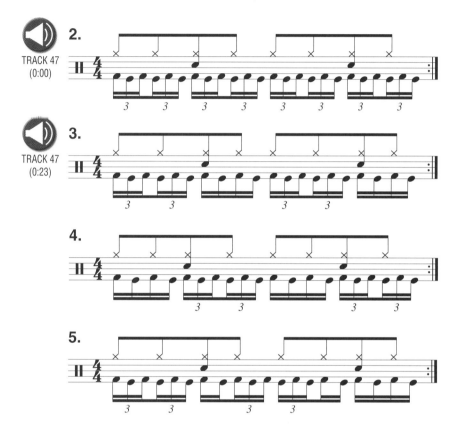

Exercise 6 uses left-foot lead on the bass drums. The left foot plays eighth notes and the right foot fills in the triplets. Exercise 7 is the same, except the left foot bridges the bass and hi-hat pedals.

6.

L R R L R R L R R L R R L R R L R R L R R L R R

TRACK 47
(0:41)

7.

L R R L R R L R R L R R L R R L R R L R R L R R

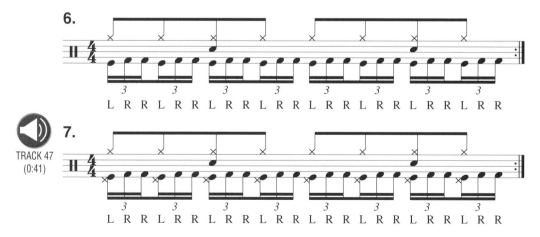

DOUBLE BASS DRUM FILLS

Use this four-measure phrase to practice the following double bass drum fills. Stickings are written above the crashes.

TRACK 48
Phrase,
Ex. 4, 7, 8

Phrase

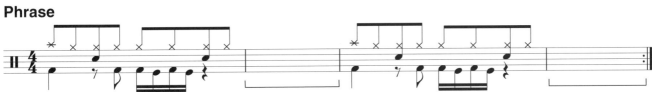

Insert a fill from below in the blank measures above.

6 FOOT PATTERNS

The key to learning any foot pattern, in this book or elsewhere, is to gradually build independence over the feet, meaning the feet need to be able to play their own pattern no matter what the hands are doing. To achieve this, one must first learn the basics over the feet and build from there. After learning to play a foot pattern by itself, refer to the list below, which shows a recommended order for practice with the hands.

1. Reading Material
2. Accent Patterns
3. Rudiments
4. Drum Beats
5. Fills and Soloing

Practicing in this way, in the above order, will build independence, and at the same time, work on technique, timing, and coordination. Any of the reading pages, accent exercises, rudiments, rock beats, or fills can be played over the foot patterns in this chapter.

The exercises in this chapter are designed to help develop the coordination a player needs to create his or her own style. After an exercise is learned, it needs to be personalized with crashes, flams, and/or toms.

Pedal bridging can also be used on any foot pattern in this chapter. There is one more idea to consider when using pedal bridging: bass drum sizes. Ginger Baker's signature style was to have two different size bass drums. His right bass drum was a 20", and he used a larger 22" drum as his left bass. Kofi has adopted this style, but has reversed the sizes so the larger drum is on the right side. This is an interesting idea because it creates two separate tones. The same effect can be created with two bass drums of the same size by tuning them to separate pitches. Also try using two different types of beaters with a double bass drum pedal.

TRIPLET FOOT PATTERNS

The first foot pattern in this chapter is a triplet foot pattern. The hi-hat foot plays quarter notes and the bass drum plays every third note of the triplet. Practice this foot pattern by itself until it is comfortable, then move on to the Reading Exercise. (Pedal bridging may also be used on any foot patterns in this chapter.)

1.

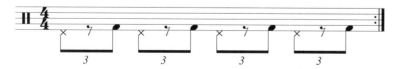

2.

3.

Exercise 3 is an Afro-Cuban pattern, like that from Chapter 4.

Although the Triplet Reading Exercise is notated with the foot pattern in Exercise 1, Track 49 plays Exercise 3, the Afro-Cuban pattern. Practice this exercise and others in the chapter with all foot patterns.

TRACK 49

Triplet Reading Exercise

RUDIMENTS

The next exercises consist of several rudiments written over the triplet foot pattern. Practice the other rudiments from Chapter 2 with this triplet foot pattern as well.

1. Double Stroke Roll

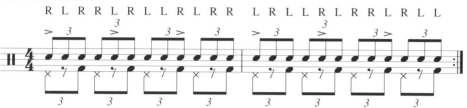

2. Five and Seven Stroke Rolls

3. Paradiddle

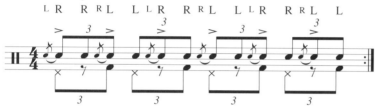

4. Flam Tap

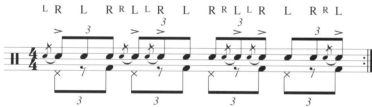

5. Pataflafla

QUARTER-NOTE TRIPLETS WITH RIGHT HAND

In this section, the right hand plays quarter-note triplets, while the feet play the triplet foot pattern. In the Pattern, the right hand is on the low tom. This leaves the left hand free to solo around the drums.

Floor Tom Pattern

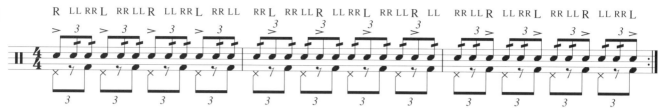

Play Exercises 1–6 with the left hand while playing the Floor Tom Pattern above. Track 51 plays an exercise first (which includes the Floor Tom Pattern), followed by one bar of only the Floor Tom Pattern, then moves onto the next exercise, each time playing the Floor Tom Pattern by itself, in between the exercises.

1.

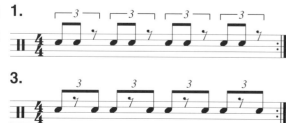

2.

3.

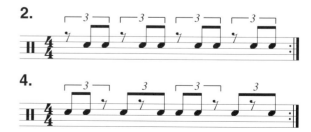

4.

5.

6.

In Exercise 7, the right-hand quarter-note triplets are on the cymbal. Three distinct grooves are created just by altering the left-hand snare placement. The exercise starts out in a 6/8 feel, changes to cut time, and ends up feeling like a 4/4 rock beat. The triplet foot pattern stays the same throughout the exercise.

TRACK 51
(0:31)

7.

LATIN DRUMMING

Foot Patterns

The second foot pattern in this chapter is the Latin Foot Pattern. The basic pattern is shown in Exercise 1. Exercises 2 and 3 are variations. Practice the foot patterns by themselves until they feel comfortable, then move on to the Drum Beats.

Drum Beats

All the Latin Drum Beats are written with the foot pattern in Exercise 1. Also practice these beats using Exercises 2 and 3. The left-hand snare part has been left out of Exercises 4 and 5. Learn the cymbal line against the foot pattern first. Then, use the Melody Line Reading exercises from Chapter 3 as a snare drum part for Exercises 4 and 5.

4.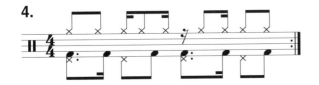

5.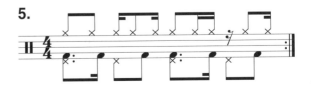

Track 52 plays Latin Drum Beat 6, and ends with Latin Fill 1 from the upcoming section titled "Fills."

TRACK 52

6. Rhumba Clave (2-3) on Snare Drum

7. Son Clave (2-3) on Snare Drum

8.

9.

Accents and Rudiments

The following are some exercises to help improve independence. In Exercise 1, the accents are on the toms. Exercise 3 has flam accents moving down and up the toms. The sticking uses left-handed flams to move down the drums, and right-handed flams to move back up. For drum kits with more than three toms, extend the exercise so the flam accents go down and up all the drums.

1. Accents

2. Double Paradiddle (with two accents)

3. Flam Accents

To further work on independence over the Latin Foot Pattern, practice the Sixteenth-Note Accent Exercises in Chapter 1 and all of the Rudiments.

Fills

The following two fills can work well with the Latin Foot Pattern.

The fill in Exercise 1 is played at the end of Track 52, which features Beat 6, "Rhumba Clave (2-3) on Snare Drum" from the previous section on Latin drum beats.

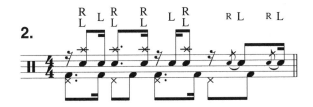

SAMBA DRUMMING

Foot Patterns

The samba foot pattern, shown in Example 1, is similar to the Latin foot pattern. Example 2 is a variation in which the hi-hat with foot plays upbeat eighth notes instead of quarter notes.

Drum Beats

The Samba drum beats are written with the foot pattern from Example 1. Practice all the beats using the variation from Example 2 as well. Exercises 3 and 4 do not have a left-hand snare part notated. Learn the cymbal line against the foot pattern first. Then, use the Melody Line Reading sections from Chapter 3 as a snare drum part for Exercises 3 and 4.

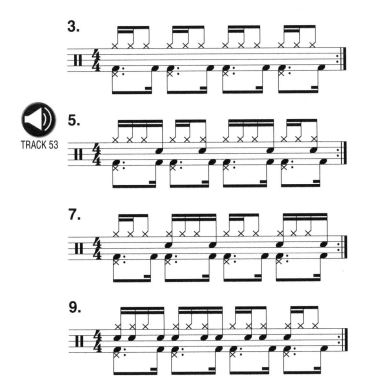

THREE AGAINST FOUR (3:4)

The next section of this chapter will focus on the Three-Against-Four foot pattern.

Foot Pattern

This foot pattern was introduced earlier in the book in the Rock Beats in 3/4 section. The hi-hat with foot plays three evenly spaced notes while the bass drum plays four evenly spaced notes in the same measure. This is why it is called "Three Against Four." We may refer to this, when two different meters are being played at the same time, as a "polyrhythm." This particular polyrhythm may be written with a colon, such as "3:4."

3:4 Polyrhythm

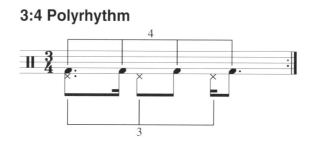

Practice this foot pattern by itself at first. The key to this or any other foot pattern is to have the feet be on "autopilot." With practice, the foot pattern will become second nature, allowing the concentration to be on what the hands are playing. To gain this level of independence, one must first start with simple coordination exercises, and gradually build up to more complex patterns. After the 3:4 foot pattern can be played comfortably, move on to the reading exercises that follow.

Reading Exercise in Eighth Notes

Reading Exercise in Sixteenth Notes

Accent Patterns

In addition to playing the accented patterns as written, try moving the accented notes to different toms or cymbals.

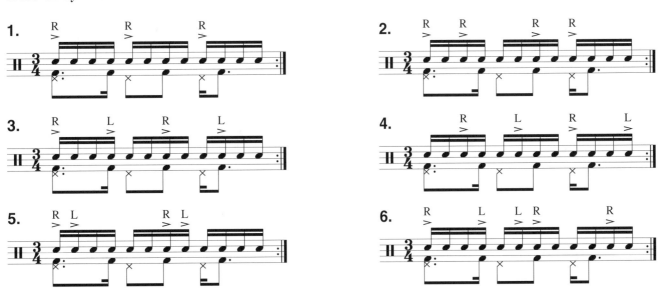

Rudiments

As with the other foot patterns in this chapter, the rudiments need to be practiced over the 3:4 foot pattern also. The rudiments that are in 3/4 time work best, but any of them can be played over this foot pattern. Here are some examples.

1. Double Stroke Roll

2. Seven Stroke Roll

3. Double Paradiddle

4. Flam Accent

5. Single Flammed Mill

Exercise 6 demonstrates the idea of "playing off of the four." The paradiddle can be played in a "three" or a "four feel." In the first two measures, the paradiddles are in a "three feel." The accents line up with the hi-hat with foot. In the last two measures, the paradiddles change to a "four feel." The accents line up with the bass drum. This makes the paradiddles seem to speed up. The tuplet "16:12" is used because sixteen notes are played in the place of twelve.

TRACK 54

6. Paradiddles

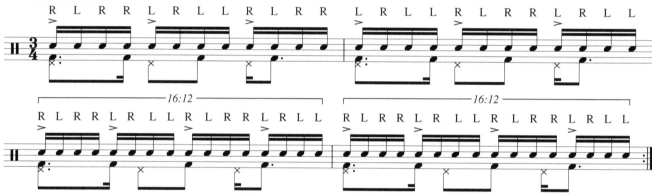

Drum Beats

The following are some examples of different drum beats over the 3:4 foot pattern.

1. 3:4 (3 on the hi-hat; 4 on the bass drum)

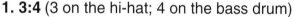

2. 3:4 (3 on the bass drum; 4 on the hi-hat)

3. 3:4 (3 on the hi-hat; 4 on the bass drum)

4. 3:4 (3 on the hi-hat; 4 on the bass drum)

5. 6/8 Feel

6. Tom Beat or Fill

Exercise 7 places a shuffle hand pattern over the 3:4 foot pattern. Doing this shifts the feel to the "4" on the bass drum. The snare hits line up with the bass drum. It feels like playing in 4/4, with quarter notes on the bass drum. Try playing back and forth between Exercise 1 and Exercise 7 to feel the beat shift from a three-feel in Exercise 1 to the four-feel in Exercise 7. There is also an example of this switch in the Solo Exercise in the next section.

TRACK 55
Ex. 7, 8

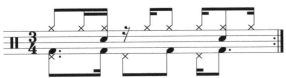

Solo Exercise—3:4 Foot Pattern

This solo exercise combines many ideas over the 3:4 foot pattern. Learn it one line at a time and then put the entire solo together. Pay close attention to the measures 7–8: the foot pattern changes so that the "4" is on the hi-hat, and the "3" is on the bass drum. The snare also moves to the "ands" of beats 2 and 3.

3:4 Foot Pattern in 4/4

Here is another way of playing the 3:4 foot pattern. Instead of it being in 3/4 meter like the previous exercises, the foot pattern is now in 4/4. When playing the pattern in 4/4, a quarter-note triplet is used for the 3, and eighth notes for the 4. Exercise 1 shows the 3:4 pattern in 4/4.

1.

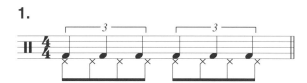

The easiest way to get the feel of playing this foot pattern is by using sixteenth-note triplets on the snare drum. Both the hi-hat eighth notes and the bass drum quarter-note triplet line up with sixteenth-note triplets. In the Exercises 2–4, the notation has the feet connected up to the hands to show which notes line up together.

The hi-hat foot in Exercise 2 is playing eighth notes and lines up on every third sixteenth-note triplet.

2.

Exercise 3 includes the bass drum, which lines up with every fourth sixteenth-note triplet.

3.

Exercise 4 is the same as Exercise 3, except crashes have been added on each bass drum hit. This exercise was introduced earlier in the book in the "Sixteenth-Note Triplet" section. This is a good fill to use as a transition into the 3:4 foot pattern.

4.

Solo Exercise—3:4 in 4/4

This solo exercise uses sixteenth-note triplet fills to transition from a 4/4 rock beat to the 3:4 foot pattern, and back to a 4/4 beat again. The fill in measure 4 sets up the foot pattern over which the hands will play. The hi-hat foot plays straight eighth notes for the entire exercise. The consistent hi-hat notes allow the hands and bass drum to shift back and forth between time feels.

TRACK 57

3:4 Hi-Hat Foot Pattern

This section explores one last idea with the 3:4 polyrhythm. The hands are playing a standard rock beat while the hi-hat foot is in a "three feel," playing once every three sixteenth notes. A polyrhythm is created since the hi-hat foot is in a 3/4 meter while hands are in 4/4. This pattern is shown in Exercise 1 below. Since the hi-hat foot is playing in 3/4, it takes three measures of 4/4 meter for the foot pattern to land on beat 1 again. Track 58 plays the exercise as written the first few times, and then adds more bass drum notes.

1.

TRACK 58
(0:00)

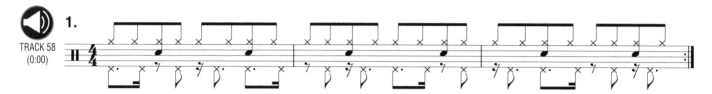

Exercise 2 includes dotted lines to show the "3/4 hi-hat foot" measures inside the three measures of 4/4.

2.

Exercises 3–6 consist of four beats to be practiced against the 3:4 hi-hat pattern. Also practice any of the other 4/4 rock beats from earlier in the book with this foot pattern.

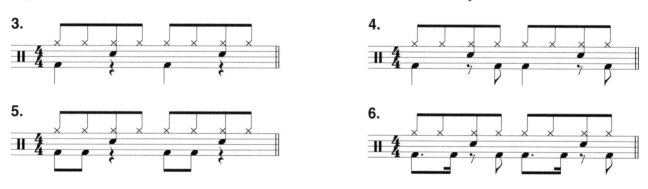

3.

4.

5.

6.

Exercise 7 is like Exercise 6, but with the 3:4 hi-hat foot pattern. Notice how the hi-hat and bass drum relate to each other: they start out playing together, shift apart, and come back together again when the pattern repeats.

7.

TRACK 58
(1:01)